CONTINUUM

Life After Death

Wilbert Smith, Jr., Ph.D.

ISBN-13: 9781537461465
ISBN: 153746146X

DEDICATION

To my Grandmother, Aslee Hall, 1892-1972.

TABLE OF CONTENTS

FORWARD

My interests in the subject of life after death, goes back to my youth and my understanding of Heaven. It was always very hard for me to understand the concept of Heaven and that if we are good people and do good deeds our reward would be in heaven and as some depicted wings and fly around for eternity, this has always been hard for me to understand because my concept has always been what do we do for eternity? I have always believed that there was a greater purpose for our souls. My understanding as a youth was that once we were in heaven there would be no work just enjoyment. My personal beliefs and that the soul did not die, only the physical body, then there must be reason for the soul to exist in the afterlife. I've always had a very strong belief in the theory of reincarnation, and my belief that this always included the total universe, because I believe there is no limit to the powers of God and by that I mean there's no reason to believe that if he created the total universe that we here on earth would be the only living entities in the universe. And in that thought I believe our souls could be reincarnated anywhere in the universe. If my understanding of the Bible is correct as we moved to the next phase after death, we will not take our thoughts and behavior to the next level with us, because for our souls and the next phase would be all of the thoughts and lifestyles we would carry the same problems that we have here and now to the next phase, and I don't believe that was the intentions of our divine ruler. Whether we reincarnate on this earth or somewhere else is not a decision that we will make and I do believe in some cases we may be back on this earth to finish unfinished missions that the supreme ruler feel that is something we must complete before we can move to the next phase. I don't believe that it will be in the same physical body because it no longer exists but it is necessary for the soul to finish its mission or whatever deed or deeds that must be fulfilled before it can move to the next level.

When I started reading literature on Metaphysical science/Religion, I said this is what I have been looking for virtually all my life, it fit my belief systems and I decided I needed to know more and I enrolled in the University of Metaphysics and to me this was one of the best decisions I've made in my life.

ACKNOWLEDGEMENT

Let me tell you a little bit about the greatness of my grandmother, Mrs. Aslee (Walker) Smith 1892-1972, to whom I dedicated this book. She had a natural connection with the Great Spirit of the Universe. She encouraged everyone she knew to embrace their natural penchant for spiritual liberation and love. Her openness to new ideas encouraged me to accept fresh initiatives and embrace creativity. She shared her gift of personal strength with me, and even though she's physically gone, she remains my mentor and guide.

CHAPTER 1
THE GATEWAY OF THE SOUL

Those, who strongly believe in the life after death, think of death as the gateway of the soul to enter the new life. Death is like a line between two half-lives; one life is lived before death and one life is lived after death. Jung (14) says that after death the soul attains the half missing life and then it reaches to the completeness. Though death is a miserable experience for the people, it is not a miserable one for the people who have studied and research death. Those, who strongly believe in life after death, think of death as the gateway of the soul to enter the new life. Death is like a line between two half-lives; one life is lived before death and one life is lived after death. Jung (14) says that after death the soul attains the half missing life and then it reaches to the completeness.

Chopra (2) calls death as a brief or temporary stopping point after which the endless journey of the soul starts. He further says that death is not the end of everything but on the contrary it opens the limitless adventures. He gives an example of a water vapour. The water drop is transformed into the vapour and this vapour is invisible, it materializes into clouds and these clouds give rain to our planet. The rivers are formed again the drop of the water merge into the sea. In this process, we cannot say that the water vapour has died on permanent basis, or its existence is extinguished. The drop is there but its form has changed. The same logic can be applied to death. The human body is like a drop of water. After death the existence does not remain solid but converts into the form of vapour and then start the unending journey of the soul from one body to another.

But still there have been debates between the scientists and philosophers regarding the existence of soul after the death of the person. There is a school of thought called naturalism. According to naturalist theory, when the person is dead; it means he/she is dead. The modern naturalism is also called as atheistic materialism or secular neutralism (Peters, 2). The naturalism says that death is the natural conclusion of life (Peter, 2). Naturalism does not accept spiritual reality. Material reality is the only reality. The medical or other physical sciences are based on naturalistic approach. If we consider the fact that there is nothing beyond material as per the naturalistic approach, many questions remain unanswered. To get the answers of those questions, we have to take support of metaphysical and spiritual science, because material or physical science is unable to answer all the questions or fulfil all curiosities that man has been encountering since the inception of life.

Physical science and naturalistic theory both have disapproved of the existence of life after death. The naturalistic people think that they are rational. This rationalism and doctrinism according to Jung (3) is a major disease. He further say that these people pretend to have the answer but they do not. While differentiating the views between science and spiritual life Jung (4) says that we do not trust the other world beyond ours; because we cannot see it or feel it. We are abided by the laws of our existing world. It shapes our mind and makes us think of this world only. This world is very limited, but we think it is the real and only world. We are brought up with so called rational thinking as science claims. But physical science is not as rational as it claims to be. Jung (4) also differentiates between scientific man and mythic man. The mythic man always craves to go beyond the finite world. He urges to know about the infinite things, but scientific man does not go beyond the infinite world and he prefers to stay. According to Jung, the perception of scientific man is very limited as compared to the mythic man.

The perceptions of the philosophers or spiritual people are different from the common man. It is because they take death in a very different way. They try to explore the mysteries of death. Here I have categorically mentioned the term spiritual or philosophers and refrain from the use 0f the word *religious*. It is because being religious makes the person constrained and he/she cannot think beyond religious rituals. Being spiritual, philosophical or metaphysical helps the person to think out of the box.

CHAPTER 2
DEATH THE UNRESOLVED MYSTERY

Death is one of the fully unresolved mysteries of the universe. The mystery has been tried to solve by people in their own way, their own comprehension. For example medical science believes that when the body dies the human existence ends. The base of medical science is on the tangible things and it does not believe those things, which cannot be comprehended with the help of our sensory organs. Beyond sensory organs nothing exists according to medical science. Like medical science, each physical science needs a concrete evidence to prove the assumptions. When we assume that there is a life after death; or the person's existence is not limited to the body, but after the end of the body, the existence remains. Scientist asks for concrete proof, if it is not there, science declares it as a null hypothesis or fake or false information. According to science, the physical existence of human is the one and only fact because you see, or touch the body. When philosophers talks about concepts of life after death, they are related to the abstract or intangible experience and there is no place for intangible elements in science. Hence there has been a debate between philosophy, spirituality and medical science. Many scholars, philosophers have collected several evidences of life after death and every time those evidences have been refuted by the scientist for not having strong concrete evidences. On this background, one more major important factor to be considered is religion. There are several stories told about life after death; but those stories are mere stories and religion is not able to give a rational answers to the questions of scientists; probably because whatever religion told, proved to be wrong in the study of science. In times past there was a belief that the sun revolved around the earth, science proved that it was not the earth but it is the sun that is steady and earth revolved around it. Such religious information once the people presumed as facts proved to be wrong by science. But when I say, several religious information was proved wrong by physical science, I mean to say "several" and not all. Some religious beliefs are there which science has not been able to prove yet and life after death is among them. Hence this book just tries to explore what different religions say about life after death; but ultimately the exploration in this book will be based on the metaphysical and philosophical attitudes about death after life.

Though the topic Life after Death, is a very abstract topics, it has been studied by several scholars from metaphysical science. Before starting our discussion, it is important to know what metaphysics is. Metaphysics is a science unlike religion. The main reason behind that is it does not compel people to trust blindly on what the scriptures or the religious people say. In religion, the person is forced to believe whatever is told in religious scripture. Metaphysical science according to Masters (38) says that it is the traditional approach of the religion that the followers of the religion must believe and accept the authority of religion; that is the Bible. But unlike the conventional authoritative approach of religion, the metaphysics never force the people to accept everything blindly. In Christianity, sainthood bestowed to a particular person has always been glorified. But it is not always true that the saint should have the knowledge of metaphysics or abstract things. On the other hand, he/she is stuck into the religious affairs. He/she thinks about the mundane world and the rituals told him/her by the Bible or any kind of religious scriptures. Moreover, he/she is inclined towards applying the biblical or scriptural examples and according to Masters, such person cannot attain the real knowledge of who we are and what the objective behind our birth is. Metaphysical science is based on the subject of experiences. Every person is different and unique; as to his experiences. He/she can experience the abstract knowledge in different ways from other people. Involving ourselves in the meaningless rituals of religion, it is more effective to take support from other spiritual activities such as meditation (Masters, 38). The authenticity of Masters' knowledge lies in his deep study of around 40 years in the field of metaphysics and philosophy. He believes in meditation, our conversation with our inner self.

When the scholars and philosophers talk about life after death, the concept of reincarnation is discussed in the circle of religion, philosophy and spiritualism as well. Though there are no scientific evidences yet found on the concept of reincarnation; there is a strong belief among the people all over the world about reincarnation. Reincarnation is the journey of soul from one tangible body to another one. "Coming back in the flesh", this is the meaning of reincarnation. The process continues till the soul attains its complete mature phase. According to the findings of Masters (44) two third of world's population believes in reincarnation; though they have different beliefs regarding reincarnation. Masters says that there are lot of misconceptions in the minds of the people regarding reincarnation. He believes that traditional religions are not able to give the precise knowledge of reincarnation. They just go on telling interesting stories which may be myths or real. Westerners are confused and reincarnation for them remains a mere biblical form. They do not take it seriously and so they are least bothered about knowing the truth behind reincarnation.

If the process of death is understood with the help of physics, most of the answers can be obtained. Masters uses the theory of energy which is told in physics. According to science the energy is the element that never perishes. The energy changes but it never ends. Science has approved the transformation of energy from one element to another. Masters (39) put the same theory forward. He says that the energy factor is accumulated outer sense of human being and during death the same outer energy is drawn inward and activates psychic sense perception. According to Masters for the rest of our life, we carry the after death existence within us in the inner level of our minds. The process of meditation can be compared with the phase during death. In meditation, the person goes inside, deep inner in his/her mind and he/she maintains contact with the astral dimension of consciousness. There are different levels in the astral dimension of consciousness.

CHAPTER 3
ASTRAL PLANES

Let's have a deep discussion in detail, how Masters has propounded the theory of life after death. While discussing the theory, Masters has stressed the term "astral planes" in which the individuals can see psychically into other dimension, or other worlds we can say which is different from our concrete world. Masters' research and study in metaphysical science is vast and through meditation, he has helped several people to visit the astral plane. Masters gives importance to the personal experience. He says that the supernatural or metaphysical experience cannot be gained in the confinement of religion. For gaining the experience, each person should be free from religious bondage. Each person is different from the other person. Masters believes that the experiences of each person are also very different so let them take their own experience about the astral plane or the world beyond this mortal world.

Masters discusses thoroughly about the life after death. He talks about some levels of astral dimension. If the person is emotionally depressed at the time of death, he/she will go to the lower dimension of astral plane. If the person is spiritually and emotionally on the higher status, the higher astral dimension will open for such person. Masters compares these levels with the higher and lower activities that we do. The person who has been hostile most of their lifetime will join the astral plane and meet the souls with similar tendencies. Masters says that we ourselves carry either heaven or hell with us. He says that our state of consciousness throughout our lifetime will decide our life after death. Through our state of mind, we decide the plane for us. In religious language, it is called heaven or hell. To the heaven, Masters calls the higher astral plane and to the hell, he calls the lower level plane. Masters (45) also explains the time span of the souls for taking rebirth. According to him, there are two types of souls; less evolved souls and highly evolved souls. Less evolved souls according the Masters take birth very frequently; that is in every century or so. The highly evolved soul on the other hand, takes birth probably after 2000 years. Masters also believes that our planet is not the only planet where the souls take birth. There are several planets that contain human life. May be these planets are more evolved than our planet and maybe the highly evolved souls take birth on the other planets for a further development process. Masters (48) also throws light on the choice of parents of the souls. According to his teachings it is in the hands of the souls to select their parents. The less evolved souls choose the parents unconsciously while the highly evolved souls choose the parents consciously.

Masters' thoughts, though cannot be proven on empirical or concrete basis, they are rational and logical. Sometimes our inner self gives us inner signals. We call it intuition. This intuition cannot be proven by giving concrete facts, but still if we listen to our inner self, our decisions and thoughts prove to be right. In Masters' teachings, it happens. It is the intuition that made me and others to accept what Masters has put forward.

Masters' ideology of life after death is similar to the ideologies that religions have put forward. Being the researcher in metaphysics, he just changed the names of physical terms. In this book, I will discuss the concepts and theories of life after death prevalent in each religion. Masters' theory of life after death seems to be similar with Eastern religious concepts of life after death.

The reincarnation is the culmination of the Karma. If the Karmas performed by human being are good and pious, it will be born according to its desire and at the same time, if the Karmas are bad, the person will be born and spend the life in a miserable condition. The Karma theory thus associated with reincarnation is nothing but a cause and effect theory. The Karmic theory has its roots in ancient Hindu, Greek, Buddhist and Egyptian philosophy. In Egyptian civilization their attitude towards death was dominated by their belief in immortality. Death is a "temporary interruption and not the cessation of life ("Egyptian Civilization - Religion - Life after Death"). The concept of mummifying the dead person were emerged from their belief that by mummifying they are opening the gate open for the next life of the person ("Egyptian Civilization - Religion - Life after Death"). The concept of reincarnation beliefs that the soul comes again in the world in the form of a completely different body. The process of reincarnation is like changing our clothes. Reincarnation according to Weiss (n.d.) is a situation or a phase where after the death of the body the personality survives and without losing the continuity, the personality embodies itself in another physical body. In short every individual is a reincarnation of past individuals (Weiss). There are some similarities found in the theory of life after death between the religious approaches and philosophical or metaphysical approaches. There are several religions, cultures and civilizations on our planet. Though the views of life after death vary, the common factor among all these religions is that they all believe in life after death. Let's start our discussion about the opinions of different religions regarding life after death.

CHAPTER 4
REINCARNATION

Reincarnation is the journey of soul from one tangible body to another one. "Coming back in the flesh", this is the meaning of reincarnation. The process continues till the soul attains its complete mature phase. The reincarnation is the culmination of the Karma. If the Karmas performed by human being are good and pious, it will be born according to its desire and at the same time, if the Karmas are bad, the person will be born and spend the life in a miserable condition. The Karma theory thus associated with reincarnation is nothing but a cause and effect theory. The Karmic theory has its roots in ancient Hindu, Greek, Buddhist and Egyptian philosophy. The concept of reincarnation opines that the soul comes again in the world in the form of a completely different body. The process of reincarnation is like changing our clothes. Reincarnation according to Weiss (n.d.) is a situation or a phase where after the death of the body the personality survives and without losing the continuity, the personality embodies itself in another physical body. In short every individual is a reincarnation of past individuals (Weiss).

The subject of life after death has been discussed in every major religion of the world. To have a thorough insight about this topic it is important to discuss what are the beliefs regarding life after death in all major religion. For this discussion, six major religions have been taken; three of them are from the west (Christianity, Muslim and Judaism) and the religions from the east especially emerged in India (Hinduism, Buddhism and Jainism).

Christians believe that there is a life even after the physical death of the person. According to them, even if the body perishes, then buried or cremated, the soul lives on and is raised to a new life by God. Jesus' death is an example of life after death. Three days after his crucifixion, Jesus was resurrected ("BBC - GCSE Bitesize: Christian Teaching"). The crucifixion of Jesus followed by his resurrection made the Christians believe that there is a life after death. There is a hope after the miseries of life.

Jesus has said, "I am the resurrection and the life,. He who believes in me will live even though he dies' (John: 11.25-26)

In the above verse of Bible, it can be said that Christianity believes that there is a life even after the death of the person. The death according to the Bible is physical death and not the death of the personality or soul.

In the second statement it is said in the Bible:

"God so loved the world that he gave his only Son, that whoever believes in him shall not perish but have eternal life". (John 3:16).

In the above statement, The Bible says that an eternal life exists even after the physical death of the person. The person has to have deep belief in God or the powerful entity that is controlling the world.

There are several debates and counter-debates related to the life after death. Religion according to scientist and atheists has no evidences to prove that there is a life after death. He will questions the religions whether they were able to prove the existence of life after death with sound experiments.

An analytical and scientific argument is done by D'Souza on the topic of life after death. According to him the human mind is not just the tangible and material force in the brain but it is an intangible component and that component in science may be called energy where as in religion it is known as the soul which survives even after the death of the person. There is a popular slogan of atheists, "The Absence of evidence is evidence of absence." It means that if there is no evidence to certain things, the things does not exist. Moreover, the scientist wants concrete proof to prove the existence of something. The atheists like Francis Crick challenges the believers that if they really believe in life after death, they should conduct a scientific test to prove it (Crick, 258).

But according to D'Souza, the scientists believe in many things which cannot be detected with the help of scientific equipment. The example is "dark matter" or "dark energy" that exists in the universe according to the scientists. D'Souza also gives an example in physics when the physicists of late 1920s had discovered the missing energy in nuclear beta-decay. At that time a hypothesis was presumed by Wolfgang Pauli that unknown particle is emitted in the reaction though the particle was not detected. D'Souza puts forward the idea that there are many such phenomena that cannot be proved concretely. Life after death is one of them.

There is theory propounded by the ancient Greek philosopher Plato; "Allegory of the Cave" It is one of the eminent and most effective attempts to elucidate the nature of reality which cannot be seen, touch or feel by outward sensory organs, but it can definitely been felt through inner forces. In his theory of "allegory of cave", Plato symbolizes cave as the mortal state of human beings. The existence of human beings in the cave symbolizes his earthly life where he thinks that whatever he sees around him is the reality and what is not seen does not exist. But when he is brought out of the cave, it is his life after death where he came to know that the world after his death is the real world and the world in which he was staying before his birth is mere hallucination. In the frenzy of scientific approach, we cannot assume that the philosopher like Plato also was not to be taken seriously. If the greatest philosophers of the world are saying positively about the death of the life and they have accepted the concept of death of life, the concept cannot be completely wrong or subject to be rejected or not to be taken seriously.

The concept of "Life after Death in Hinduism

The life after death theory is present in the ancient scriptures such as Vedas and Upanishads. In Upanishads for example, there is a verse stated by Yama; the God of Death:

"Fools dwelling in the darkness of ignorance, self-conceited with vain knowledge and puffed up with the idea that they are truly wise, go round and round like the blind led by the blind." 1 *"Hereafter never rises before the mind of an ignorant child, deluded by the desire or wealth and worldly prosperity. Such people who say: 'This is the world, there is no other,' come again and again under my sway"(Katha Upanishad 1.2.5 Chapter 1, Section 2, Verse 6)*

The God of death tells us that people have to get stuck in the cycle of birth and death. They are ignorant and they suppose that this world is everything. This is the description suitable to the people with naturalistic approach. They think that this world is the only world and beyond human body, nothing else exists. Yama called such people blind; who cannot see beyond the material things. Such people are greedy and they think themselves very knowledge-able and wise. Those people go on taking birth again and again and they do not have emancipation until they are enlightened. Here the knowledge is directly associated with the redemption from the cycle of birth and death. Hinduism tells that taking birth again and again means the soul has not yet attained the complete purity and that is why its birth and death is inevitable.

Like these verses, there are hundreds of such verses that clearly indicate that the ancient Aryans used to believe in the concept of Life after Death Theory.

CHAPTER 5

ANCIENT HINDUS AND THE CONCEPT OF HEAVEN

The ancient Hindus have a deep faith in the concept of heaven. The heaven is called (Brahmaloka) in Hinduism. Brahma + Loki; Here Brahma is the God of creation. Hindus believe that Brahma has created the universe. His abode is the place which is called heaven. The person attains Brahma Loki if his/her Karmas are good and who is the pious soul. Thus our life after death depends upon the Karmas we perform in our life. The Karma Theory is directly associated with the concept of life after death. When Aryans came to know the law of action and reaction, they started believing in the Karma Theory. Whatever you sow, you reap. This is the law of nature and the law is applicable to the cycle of death and birth as well, (Swami Abhedananda, 34).

The concept of Life after Death in Hinduism consists of four different phases or courses (Swami Adiswarananda). The first phase is Devayana. This phase is for the pure people who have lived a very pure life for all of their life. They have devoted themselves in the pious activities such as meditation. The importance of meditation discussed by Masters is the base of the Hindu philosophy of rebirth and life after death. Though they have made their life pure by sacred work and meditation, they have not yet attained the self-knowledge completely. They enter Brahmaloka, which is the highest heaven and from there after a period of time they attain liberation (Swami Adiswarananda). The second phase is called pitriyana. This phase includes the people who have done lot of donations and philanthropic activities and they are expecting the good result of the charity, worship, austerity etc. Such people enter to Chandraloka (the Lunar sphere). In this sphere, they enjoy immense happiness and pleasure for the good deeds they have performed in their earthly life (Swami Adiswarananda). But they take birth on the earth again as they have cherished the desire of rewards for their good deeds in their previous birth.

The third course is the hell. This course is for those who have been doing an immense impure life. These people have been leading a life against Dharma. After their death from previous birth, these souls take birth as sub-human species. In this life of sub-human species, their sins and impurity lessens and they again take birth as human species. The forth course is for those souls who are extremely cruel, impious and far from being improved. Such creatures take birth on the earth in forms of insects such as mosquitoes or fleas (Swami Adiswarananda). After leading the life of such mean creatures, slowly, they get elevated in their status and thus take birth as a human being. This is an opportunity given to them to elevate (Swami Adiswarananda).

In short, according to Hinduism, the life after death is far longer journey of the human soul than the life before death. The souls have to wander through different phases until their emancipation from the cycle of life.

Just like Hinduism the concept of rebirth and life after death is also found in the Quran. It is found in various Quranic verses.

> *When death comes to one of them, he says, "My Lord, send me back. I will then work righteousness in everything I left." Not true. This is a false claim that he makes. A "Bazakh"(barrier) will separate his soul from this world until resurrection (23:99-100)*

In the above verses, it is clearly mentioned that after the death of the person, God takes away his/her soul, while he/she is in process of beseech to God to get another chance for the soul to prove (Shahada). After the death, the soul goes in a barrier and it is released from the barrier only after the day of resurrection.

The second reference of reincarnation is as follows:

"They will say, "Our Lord, you have put us to death twice, and you gave us two lives; now we have confessed our sins. Is there any way out?" (40:11)

In the verse it is mentioned that the souls make covenant with the Almighty God and then again we are put to death. The second death indicates that there is a previous life which is agreed by Islam. The previous life according to Islam is our life in heaven and then we take birth on the earth. After the earthly death of the person's life, Islam believes that the angels invite the souls to re-enter heaven.

The third reference is in 28:77 where Quran explains the concept of reincarnation in the following verses.

"Use the provisions bestowed upon you by God to seek the abode of the Hereafter, without neglecting your Share in the world" 28:77

While explaining the life after death, Muslim theory of rebirth does not seem to take into consideration the Karma Theory. The following verses in the Quran say that the human being is reborn by the grace of God.

God has given a share to every human being on this earth and this life is decided by God's will. It has no connection with his previous life. But here also Islam has mentioned previous life.

The above religious verses from the Quran indicate that this religion agrees that there is a life after death.

Judaism also propounds the life after death theory. Judaism says that there is a soul within the body and at the time of death, the soul leaves the body and enters heaven for refreshment ("BBC - GCSE Bitesize: Judaism And Death"). There is a rest for a week which is known as Sabbath G-d (God) offers an extra soul to everyone. The Jewish people also believe that after death, the person goes to Sheol ("BBC - GCSE Bitesize: Judaism and Death"). Sheol is a dark place where the souls stay for eternity. The concept of life after death is described in the following genesis.

"Many of those who sleep in the dusty earth will awaken: these for everlasting life and these for shame, for everlasting abhorrence" (Daniel, 12.2). The concept of heaven and hell is there like other religions. Judaism tells us that the pious and virtuous people will attain the place called Gan Eden; which means paradise, while the impious and evil people will have to lead a miserable life in Gehenna; which is hell. The people tend to be confused between Gehenna and Sheol as Sheol is the dark place and hell also is the dark place; but there is difference between these two places. Sheol is the place for the waiting phase of the soul until its judgement day, whereas Gehenna is hell where the judgement of the soul has already been completed and they have been sent to the place to lead a punished and miserable life. Life after death according to Judaism is in the hands of G-d ("BBC - GCSE Bitesize: Judaism and Death").

After studying the opinions from the major religions of the world regarding life after death, one fact is clear is that all religions have agreed that there is a life after death. One common fact is that no religion states that physical death is the end of life. All religions tend to agree with the fact that there is something more than a mere physical body which cannot be overlooked. The quote of Hick is mentioned by Donnelly (265), 'Any religious understanding of human existence – not merely one's own existence but the life of humanity as a whole positively requires some kind of immortality belief and would be radically incoherent without it.

On the perspectives of physical sciences, there is no strong evidence for all these stories. They are myths and science supposed them irrational and illogical. Yet the religions from the world have not been able to give concrete proofs to these stories. These are the traditional stories and are supposed as mere legends. That is why it has become necessary to prove the assumption that life exists after death

CHAPTER 6

THE THREE DEATHS IN BUDDHISIM

According to Buddhism, though the life span of every individual is different, ultimately everyone has to die. According to Buddhism life never starts with birth and ends with death (Dao). Buddhism believe that we were living before this life and we will live after this life as well. Death is the simple phenomenon. It is just the end of one life and beginning of another life. The major problem is the suffering which we gain in every life. Buddhism has accepted three types of death:

1. In the first type of death, Buddhism tells us that the length of the life is not important; but the important thing is the Karmas. When our past Karmas will end, we will stop to live. For example the lamp glows till the fuel is gone. Once the fuel is over the lamp stops glowing.
2. Everyone's lifespan is different. Buddhism believe that some of us die before getting old; it is because of the exhaustion of merit.
3. Third type of death occurs due to various calamities such as wars, earthquake, flood or any such natural or manmade disasters.

Whatever cause may be everyone has to face death. No one has escaped from it. Unlike Hinduism, Buddhism does not think that the Karmas from previous life influence our current life; but the actions which are taken in our present life are also responsible for the different incidents of our life. But like Hinduism, Buddhism also say the same thing and that is "as you sow will reap". Three major situations of Karmas have been described by Buddhism.

1. Strong Karma: During the death of the person, the good or bad karmas appear in front of the eyes of the dying person. The strong thoughts; may be good or evil will determine our future. Here Buddhism wants to say that if we want the

life after death to be peaceful and tranquil, our thoughts during our death need to be pious and virtuous.

2. The first situation was for those who have done either good or evil karmas. But there are some people, who have not done either good or evil karmas. Their Karmas are neither too good nor too bad. In such situation, the person gets minor reward for his minor good deeds and minor punishment for the minor evil deeds.

3. The last thought in Buddhism is very important. If the last thoughts comes in the mind of the human being is pious and virtuous it will lead him/her a peaceful death and a good rebirth; but if the thoughts during our death are impure and full of hatred, it will badly impact on our rebirth. Hence Buddhism always encourages to the ill and dying people to have good thoughts in their mind during the last breathing of their life. It will assure them a peaceful death and good future in next rebirth. Buddhism encourages having Buddha's name on their mouth, and Buddha's thoughts in their mind.

According to Buddhism crying at the time of death is also not good for the dying person as it may leave a bad impact on the emotional status of the dying person. It will lead the dying person into great misery in his/her next birth. But at the same time there is also a probability that some people have done excessive bad deeds in their life but at the time of death, if they start thinking well, and they start taking Buddha's name on their mouth, it is of no use. It is because the person's previous evil Karmas were counted and he/she will get the same punishment for those evil deeds. The person will hardly get a good rebirth.

Buddhism says that along with Karma one more important thing is the defilements which are the other cause of rebirth. The people who are greedy all the time and who have excessive attachment for the world pleasures are likely to be in the cycle of birth and death continuously. Thus the simple teaching of Buddhism about rebirth and life after death is that there is a life after death and if one wants to have good fortune; a good rebirth, he or she has to do good things in their life from detaching ourselves from the process of life and death and ultimately attain the salvation.

To conclude, we can say that Buddhism believes in life after death. It believes that the good deeds always assure good rewards and for bad deeds one has to pay and lead a miserable life. Buddhism believes in the theory of Karma and the overall approach of a human being. It says that the rebirth is based on the action. It believes in action and reaction theory like the Hindu theory explained in Vedas and Upanishads. It seems to be acceptable because no one in the world is perfect and everyone is bound to make some or other wrong deeds in their lives. Hence it is rational to perceive reward for good and punishment for bad.

Buddhism and Jainism are the two religions emerged from Hinduism; hence most of their opinions are somewhat similar with each other. Jainism like other similar Asian religions (Hinduism and Buddhism) believe that there is a birth after the death and the next birth depends upon the Karmas. Let's review the views of Jainism regarding life after death. Jainism states that everything is impermanent and subject to perish at the same time the new things are born. Life-death, creation-destructions are the law of nature. Jainism believes that when the soul will escape from its Karmas ("Jainism Simplified Chapter 4 - Gati"), it will be free. Till then it has to travel through the cycle of birth and death. Jainism strongly believes in the impact on Karmas on the existing life and future life of human beings. It strongly offer for consideration that there is no God who decides our future; but it is our Karmas.

CHAPTER 7
JANISIM FOUR DESTINIES

J ainism has given four destinies of human life after death ("Jainism Simplified Chapter 4 - Gait"). First destiny is the Human Being. As human beings, we are endowed with so many precious gifts by God and one of the most precious gift given to us by God is our intellectuality and the consciousness. Jainism says that we should control and restrict our life with certain rules and practice those rules in the whole of our life. Like Buddhism, Jainism also encourages renunciation of worldly pleasure and embrace monkhood and this leads to the salvation of the soul.

The second destiny of the soul is the heavenly being. Jainism also discusses about heavenly life which gives the soul lot of pleasure and luxuries though this life also has some limitations. Jainism says that heavenly life is momentary and it is subject to end. The end of this life brings lot of miseries in the life of the person. So instead of adopting heavenly pleasure, Buddhism recommends the life of the monk and nuns,

The third destiny of the soul narrated by Jainism is the Tiryanch being. Tiryanch means the birth not as a human being, but as an animal, bird or plant. This life is generally regarded as the lower life. It is because these living beings have given brain and intellectuality; but that is only for their survival. They cannot think beyond that. They cannot differentiate between good and bad, right and wrong. Hence they have to go through lot of miseries and sorrows throughout their lives. This life of the soul never brings him towards salvation. For the salvation of the soul, a constrained, balanced human life is necessary according to Jainism.

The fourth destiny of the soul according to Jainism is the infernal being. Infernal being leads a very dreadful life which is called the life in hell. The souls in this life lead a miserable life beyond imagination. In the hell like place, these soul constantly fight with each other and it makes their lives full of sufferings. That is why this life is also not at all suitable for the spiritual elevation of the soul.

These four destinies of the souls are as Gati in Jainism. The above discussion, it can be inferred that there is only one Gati which is suitable for the soul to gain salvation and redemption and that the human being. Jainism discusses a lot about the Karmas and their impact. The qualities and personalities of the people from hell is described in Jainism. Such people from hell are involved in continuous violence, stealing, and robbing, lying and excessive sensuous pleasures. They are egoistic, greedy, and angry and they are not ready at all to give up their worldly life. Such people are likely to born as the infernal beings.

Unlike the infernal beings, there are good souls. They are simple, balanced, disciplined. They observe vows and they have gained the ability to control their lives. Such people are always keen to gain true knowledge that always lead a moral life. Such people live as a heavenly being after death.

The souls from Hell had lived their life as greedy human beings and they wish evil about other people, they are born as animals or the lower level human beings.

Those who are simple, straightforward and they always follow the path of truth. They do not have a strong attachment towards worldly pleasures; they have control on their emotions such as anger, greed or deception. They generally take birth as human beings.

In short, Jainism believes in Karmas. The Gati (Destiny) of human beings depends upon his Karma and his next birth is also determined by his Karmas. The approach of Jainism towards life after death seems to be linear. It does not answer several questions. While talking about Karmas and their consequences, Jainism has only said that either human beings are good or bad. Either soul is involved in good deeds or bad deeds. Jainism has not taken into consideration the combination of human beings. It means that maximum human beings in the world are not fully good or virtuous; nor are they completely bad or evil. The human personality is the mixture of good and bad qualities. For example, the greedy person may have some good qualities in his personalities that are suitable for the human destiny or heavenly destiny. Jainism does not answer this question. It does not tell what happens with those who neither have complete dark shade or white shade to their personality. Hence the concept of Life after Death in Jainism seems to be inadequate.

After studying the doctrine of all major religions regarding life after death, one factor is common and that is Karma. Every religion believes in Karma theory. Only religious views cannot be enough but the concept of life after death needs to be described through metaphysical perspectives as well. Many metaphysical scholars have perceived the theory life after death differently. Masters for example, has given importance to meditation. To comprehend metaphysical things such as Life after Death, it is essential to have a deep meditation practice according to Masters (45). It is like a movie with several flashback incidents. It is just like we have some memories of past life with us and we remember them in our conscious status. The memories of past life can be recalled with the help of a deep unconscious level.

CHAPTER 8

SCIENTIFIC RESEARCH OF LIFE AFTER DEATH

The last question 0f our discussion is how we can say that life after death exists. For exploring this question, this paper conducts previous research of different metaphysical scientists and philosophers. In the beginning of this paper, we said that science has not fully agreed to the concept of life after death, but now medical science has partially accepted the term life after death. There are many researches being conducted on the topic, life after death. News regarding the largest research conducted by medical science on the topic of life after death, this medical study has been conducted with 2000 people who were admitted in 15 hospitals in the United States, the United Kingdom and Australia. In the --results, some shocking facts were revealed. The researcher found that nearly 40% of the people who survived tells their experience about their awareness during the time when they were medically declared dead. Their hearts restarted (Knapton). Among them one man narrated the story of his own resurrection. He said that he could watch his own body from a distance.

He was separated from his body completely. The shocking thing was that the man described everything happening in the room during the time when he was declared dead. The cardiac patients were studied, among them 39% of them experienced some kind of awareness when they were actually dead from the doctors' point of view (Knapton). Among them, one patient said that an unusual feeling of peacefulness was experienced. One third of the declared dead patients said that they felt that the time had slowed down or it went fast. Some of them also said that they experienced light; golden flash or the sun shining. Others felt that they had the feeling of drowning in very deep water. 13% of them said that they felt as if they were being separated from their bodies (Knapton). According to Dr.Parnia, the others may be away from such feelings due to the drug or sedatives (Knapton). Dr. Parnia shared one of the cases in Independent that a 57-year-social worker died for a while and during this phase; he was able to see what was happening in the room. Dr. Parnia said, "He seemed very credible and everything that he said had happened to him had actually happened" (Withnall). These experiences which the people gained were those experiences when they were declared actually dead by the doctors. This empirical study is the big evidence of the life after death. It clearly indicates that there is something after the death. It is certainly not as the scientist generally perceives.

Human beings generally tends to accept the facts that come from the experts, who have immense credentials. A Harvard trained neurologist has conducted a lot of research in the area of life after death. His name is Dr. Eben Alexander (Brancaz). He did experiments and came up with the conclusion that there is life after death. Before the experiment and the study, he did not believe in the life after death. He was surrounded by the medical background and material and concrete evidences. This shaped his mind for being a non-believer of the concept of life after death. He would think that the concept of a soul is eccentric and hard to believe. Dr. Alexander completely changed his perception after an incident happened with him. It was an incident when he was in coma for seven days. It was because of the severe bacterial meningitis. In the phase of his coma, he went through the surprising experience (Brancaz). He visited both heavenly and less heavenly sphere. When he returned to his body, he experienced an amazing healing experience. He came up with his opinion that our life is just a test and it is given to us to evolve and grow (Brancaz).

According to Fechner (xv), our bodies are just like wavelets on the surface of the earth as leaves grow upon a tree and our consciousness arises out of the whole earth consciousness. It makes us forget the whole background of experience; but when it sinks into the background of forgetfulness, it leads to a freer life (Fechner, xvi). Fechner (1) explains what birth is and what death is. According to him, human being stays in this world three times. His life has three different stages according to Fechner (1), in the initial stage of its existence, man stays alone in the darkness (Fechner, 1). His second stage is spent in the company of the others. In the third stage the life of the person is merged with other souls into the Supreme Spirit. He further explains the evolution of human life. In the first stage the life is formed from the germ and evolves for the second phase. In the second phase the spirit unfolds from the seed-bud and obtains the power for the third phase. In the third phase a divine spark is developed that exists in every human soul. The journey of the person from first stage to second stage is called birth and its journey from the second to third is called death according to Fechner (2). While expressing his belief in life after death, Fechner (10) says that the things that we as human beings have contributed during our life of creation, preservation will continue to work even after our destruction.

Weiss (101) also agrees with life after death. Reincarnation is the culmination of life after death. The study of reincarnation has been conducted by the social scientists as well. For example, Weiss (103) has referred to the study of Dr. Ivan Stevenson who was the researcher and psychiatrist from the University of Virginia. Dr.Stevenson has collected immense empirical data regarding reincarnation. But his data regarding life after death could not be complete; and just on the basis of that data one cannot conclude that there is life after death. This is because of some of the reasons.

The first reason is that Stevenson collected the information by observing young children. It is hard to verify the information he has obtained from the children. His cases did not include the experience of the adults. Hence it seems to be inadequate data. Second reason is that it is very difficult to find such children who know their past life. They are very rare. We generally do not find such people in the whole of our life; who had undergone through such experiences and especially the children. The third reason is that in Stevenson's cases consisted of death through young age and violence. If the children are rare to find, how could it be possible to collect the data? If Stevenson claims that these children have come again on the earth with reincarnation, why this has happens to these rare children only and why other normal and all children do not have such kind of experiences. Generally in research, the sample size of the similar population is taken for study and research. The sample size represents the whole population. But Stevenson's research and data collection does not fulfil the condition of data collection. The sample size selected by him does not represent the population. These are very rare children. The question then arises whether few of children have been studied who are very rare, is it plausible to jump to certain conclusions. Hence Stevenson's research cannot be the complete answer to the theory of life after death.

There are five different theories of incarnation stated by Weiss (n.d.);

According to the first theory of incarnation, every personality is the reincarnation of other past personality (256). It means that the personality of each individual is connected to the other personalities of his past births. There are series of events occurring in current life. If such types of incidences have been experienced by the individual in his/her previous birth, the existing life of an individual can get the access to those memories in the past.

The second theory of Weiss (257) propounds that the reincarnation is a continuous process of personality without the physical continuity. This theory was propounded by the old school of Buddhism. That says that the personality remains the same but it changes the body. The personality transfers from one body to another. The new birth takes place after the proper circumstances arise. These circumstances are suitable for the personality and then the conception happens. The obtained new body is completely different from the old one, but the personality remains the same. Moreover the circumstances have also been changed so it is difficult for the personality to suit with the new body and the new environment. Commonly we find that if there are siblings, they are not necessarily like each other. Sometimes there is a polar distance between the personality, behaviour and approach of the two brothers or sisters. The upbringing of these siblings is done by the same mother and family members; but there is a vast difference between their personalities. Now the question is whether the impact of upbringing is there on shaping certain personalities of the individual. In such case we can apply the second theory of reincarnation as continuity of personality without physical continuity.

Sometimes there are birthmarks on the human body. They may have their connection with the previous birth according to Weiss. It can be caused due to a fatality that happens with the person in his previous birth.

The third theory of Weiss is the personality survival which directly leads to the incarnation. There are three stages. The first stage is called "transition stage". In this stage Weiss (258) says that it is a stage where the physical dead body is ready for the funeral process. In this stage the communication of the dead person with the alive relatives stops. In the second stage, the personality lives near the environment where he/she has died. The third stage involves choosing parents for the next birth.

The forth theory described by Weiss (260) is Partial Reincarnation. In the theory Weiss (261) has given some cases of partial reincarnation. He describes his first case as follows:

There was an eighteen years boy who used to write poetry. He was also interested in playing music and he used to compose songs as well. Unfortunately the boy was killed in an accident. His heart was donated to an eighteen years old girl; called Danielle. After a year the donor came to the parents of the boy. The parents played some music which was composed by their dead son. The girls was hearing the composition for the first time. She did not know anything about the song. But as the music started she started to say the lines ahead and thus she completed the song.

Another case described by Weiss (261) in which a forty-seven-year-old person received a heart of a forty-year-old woman. She was a gymnast and she had a problem with eating disorders. After the heart transplantation, the man started eating disorders.

When medical science claims that the heart is a emotionless organ. When in truth it is one of the organs of body which is controlled by our brain. Doctors also say that the feelings and emotions come from brain and not heat. In poetry or art, the heart is of great importance. It is supposed to be the symbol of love and affection. The above both cases have proved that the heart is not emotionless but something abstract stays within the heart. Weiss calls it personality. The personality that stays within the heart remains there even after the heart is transplanted from one body to another.

In the fifth theory Weiss (262) talks about soul based theories of reincarnation. The soul is known by different names such as spirit, mind, consciousness, self and personality as used by Weiss. In the theosophical studies, the term soul is coined as the casual body. In most of the cases, the decay of physical body is followed by a sojourn and during this time the hell and heaven both are experienced by the person (Weiss, 265-266). The emotions of pervious life are still there to influence the personality. The personality plays with these emotions for a certain period. But this phase is temporary. Eventually this vital body also dies followed by a mental body which also dies. The experiences still remains into the soul and eventually the soul gets ready for reincarnation.

In Berlin a thorough study was conducted by the team of psychologists as well as medical doctors and came up with the conclusion that life after death exists. They have conducted the research regarding the people with near death experiences. Among these experiences, the very common experience is the detachment from body, feeling of security, love, warm and levitation (Holden, Greyson and James). In the experience of detachment of life the person feels that he/she is getting separated from the physical body. The people can actually feel and see their physical body from distance. Some of the people felt very secure; more secure than their physical life. Some people also told that they experience a very amazing feeling of divine love when they left their physical body. There is a medical practitioner in India called Dr. Vartak. He has written a book called rebirth. In the book, Dr. Vartak reveals his own experience that his wife died due to cancer. In the last days of her life, she suffered a lot. Her body was getting perished day by day. After her death, one day Dr. Vartak saw his wife, he was astonished to see her because she was looking very happy; far happier when she was alive. Dr. Vartak said that he had never seen her happy before. He wanted to say that the happiness on her face was divine. It was very different from the mundane world.

The research also revealed the fact that these people experienced absolute dissolution and a presence of overwhelming light.

Masters (38) has given many such cases in which the person literary felt the existence of two existences in the same body; the physical existence and the astral existence of a human being. He tells that the people who are undergoing surgery, experience that they have come out of their physical body and they could watch what was happening in the operation room. In the Berlin case study as well as Master's above example, there is no satisfactory answer or explanation with science. The person in the operation room is unconscious. During surgery, the patient is first given anaesthesia, and then the operation starts. It is not possible for the person to tell what is happening around him/her when he/she is under the influence of anaesthesia. Then how the person could tell exactly what was happening around him and with his physical body. Hence medical science is inadequate to answer these questions.

In one case, one of his students explained him a thrilling experience (Masters, 42). While driving the car, the student lost control of the car and his car collided with another car. He came to know then that the accident was inevitable and to his surprise he suddenly found himself alongside the highway; not with his physical body, but with his psychic, astral body. He could see what was happening with his physical body. When the two cars smashed with each other, his physical body flew forth from the car and crashed to the pavement. Then he found himself again in his physical body. It was as if God had decided that his actual death time had not yet come and that is why he ordered his astral body to enter his physical body again. It was a very mysterious experience which the student explained.

The Berlin case studies and the experience narrated by masters' student are the two cases that can be the evidences to prove that there is a life after death. It also makes clear that physical body is not everything but beyond that there exists another body. These experiences cannot be said to be totally wrong, but science should accept the challenge and try to explore the facts within these experiences. Disapproving abstract phenomena just because they have no concrete evidences is not a good idea. Instead scientist should expand their periphery and limit their tendency of relying on concrete facts.

In one such case happened with me which I (Dr. Masters) would like to share. I had joined a coaching for the study of astrology. It was just as a hobby. One day, our teacher told all the students to share the unusual experience if they had in their life. One of the students told her of her experience which was thrilling and dreadful. She was just married and she came to her husband's house. It was a joint family and the house was very huge with a well at the back side. One day, when she was alone she saw a man near the well. He was mysterious and unknown to her. She asked him who he was and he did not answer. After that she frequently could see the man everywhere, in her kitchen, bedroom hall, and out of the house as well. Initially it was very frightening experience for her. She even tried to tell about the man to her family members but all of them overlooked her saying that she might be having hallucination. Gradually she became used to the person. If she could not see him any of the days, she would become restless. After some time, they moved to the new apartment and then the man disappeared from her sight and from her life. After hearing her story, our teacher asked her whether she tried to communicate with the person. Actually she tried, but the man never responded to her. Later on she came to know that the man was the owner of the house in which they were living. He had no issues so he promised his faithful servant that he would offer that property to him. The servant became greedy and he murdered his master. He buried the body at the place outside the house near the well. Later on the house was demolished and a new building was constructed there. The builder allotted the space for shops as well and some shops were constructed there. But today there is a shop in which not a single business can be run. If someone starts any business, it cannot succeed. It was because the shop was constructed on the same place where the owner was buried.

This is the real story told by our close friend. She is not good at all in creating stories. But whatever she told was true. For verifying her experience, we went to see the place of the shop. It was closed. We asked the other shopkeepers. They told the same thing.

This story tells us that there is a life after death. The man was alive in the form of his astral body which seemed to be real. He might have some unfulfilled desires which were not allowing him to leave this finite world.

In short many such evidences are there that can prove that there is a life after death. Many people have narrated their experiences regarding Life after Death. Some decades ago, it was fashionable to mock the spirituality and the theory of life after death. People used to take them just for their entertainment. It was a trend developed among the scientists and atheists that there is no such phenomenon which can be called life after death (Leadbeater, 2). But now, many scientists have started showing interest in this area. Leadbeater (2, 3) has given testimonies and evidences to prove the fact that even rational minded people also have now accepted life after death, though everyone's perception is different. The first evidence Leadbeater points out is that some of the scientists showed keenness in knowing more about life after death are Sir William Crookes. Crookes is the inventor of Crookes's radiometer, and metal thallium. Sir Oliver Lodge; who was an eminent electrician has also accepted that something is there after death and death is not the death of personality or identity of the human being. The study conducted by such great personalities is certainly welcoming. There is one more testimony that can be given as the evidence of life after death and that is the modern spiritualism, which emerged in 1848. The modern spiritualism became popular not just because it was entertaining and ensured comfort to the people but because it's motto was to combine the empirical methods and discoveries of science (like invisible force of electricity) with the religious ideas of life after death ("BBC - Religions - Spiritualism: History Of Modern Spiritualism"). The third evidence is the theophysical evidence which means the direct investigation. It means that every human being is unique so as his experiences. Human beings have hidden senses among themselves. Through these senses, the abstract world can be accessed.

CHAPTER 9

CONCEPTIONS, APPROACHES AND VIEWS OF LIFE AFTER DEATH

As mentioned before, there are several conceptions, approaches and views regarding life after death. The conceptions are sometimes based on the individual experiences or sometimes they are based on the spiritual and metaphysical conceptions, while sometimes they are purely influenced by the religious teaching in which the person is brought up. According to Leadbeater (6) the person does not change at all after his/her death. He/she remains the same person. His intellectual capacity remains the same and the qualities and powers in him/her also do not change. There is no reward or punishment for his good or bad deeds according to the opinion of almost all religions. Leadbeater (7) says that "man himself/herself makes his/her own bed". The statement is the same as the religious approach of Hinduism, Buddhism or Jainism. But Leadbeater's above opinion is hard to accept that man does not change after death and remains the same. Rationally speaking it is not possible to remain the same person if the man's body perishes. Ending of physical existence itself is the transition period. If the body is cremated or buried, how can he remain the same person? His life before death is no more there with him/her, hence, rationally speaking there must be some changes in the life after death.

In the beginning of 20th century, much has been discussed regarding life after death. Yogi Ramachandra has discussed a lot about life after death, soul's awakening, astral heavens, hells, rebirth etc. According to him, the term death should be considered as the transition period of the soul and it is not a decay of the spirit. Everything in this world is subject to have a transition phase. Simple example is the example of gold. Gold after getting it from the mines are in a crude phase. It has to be processed. Sometimes the same gold is converted into beautiful jewellery. In India for example there is a tendency of people to break one piece of jewellery and convert it into another one. Sometimes the small earrings are broken and the gold is used for making a necklace. In this process, we cannot say that the gold is perished. It never perishes, but changes it form. Like that, death is a transition stage between two Great Plains of life. Yogi Ramchandra (28) says that when the person goes through this transition phase the eyesight starts being dimmer and dimmer. He further tells that in many cases the physical senses of the person start waning and the psychical senses grow gradually. Dying person gets psychically conscious and goes nearer to his loved ones who have already passed out from their lives. It is the union of the soul. And Ramchandra says that for this union, the souls do not need closeness what we perceive; i.e. physical closeness. It is because the limitations of space disappear on the Astral Plane. The soul communication according to Ramchandra is totally different from the verbal communication we, human beings do with each other. The dying person is slowly parted from his physical body. Astral body is the replica of physical body according to Ramchandra. Masters (41) also elucidates the existence of the astral body in the same way as Ramchandra describes. He says that the astral body is psychically inside the physical body during our lifetime. He further states that at the time of death, we experience that our astral body is getting separated from our physical body. Astral body is identical to the physical body (Masters, 41). Masters further states that this description is not a fraud or mere hallucination but this is a reality which has been experienced even by those who do not believe in metaphysical science or spiritual teachings.

Ramchandra further explains that initially the astral body separates from the physical body and remains there for a while. At that time, it is connected with the physical body only through a very thin and slender thread. The thread is then removes and the astral body starts floating with the soul and leaves the physical body behind it. The astral body at a certain point, carries the soul, but then the soul has to abandon the astral body as well. Thus Ramchandra tells us that both physical and astral bodies are transitory and are not permanent. After leaving the astral body, the soul plunges into a deep sleep for a certain course of time. It sleeps as if it is in a comma. It becomes prepared for rebirth. During this preparation, it accumulates strength and vigour that is required for the new phase of its existence. Like Jainism, philosophy of rebirth, Ramchandra also tells somewhat a similar theory. If the soul has departed from the physical body with no worldly attachments, its astral sleep is very peaceful. The soul takes sleep without any disturbance or any kind of sorrow or miseries. On the contrary, while leaving the physical body, if the soul is too concerned about the worldly affairs and has not detached itself from the worldly pleasures, it cannot take a peaceful sleep. The soul is always attached with the earthly concerned and it is tormented by these concerned. Its sleep is feverish.

Peters in the theological essay "Models of Life beyond Death: Comparing Concepts discusses about cybernetic immortality. This is a modern technology of separating the human soul from the body. This process can also be known as trans-humanism or post-humanism. In this process the life after death can be attained by downloading the brain activity in our computer. This is not a mere fantasy but scientists have been conducting research on it. In this research it is presumed that the human beings are centred in brain activity and brain is an abode of our personality. Our personality is exactly what our brain thinks. So the consciousness of the human being is downloaded on the computer network. Thus on the computer it would be possible to do this. There are various processes involved in trans-humanism. In the first stage; i.e. Artificial Intelligence, the human intelligence is stimulated in a robot. In the second stage, human and machine will merge in which the portion of human brain will be replaced with the mechanical parts. In stage three, the existing human intelligence will be reduced to a pattern of information processing and download it into a computer or robot. This will be the immortal intelligence life into machine which gets constant backup. This technological process is very much similar to the ancient concept of immortal soul according to Peter (5)

CHAPTER 10
CONCLUSIONS AND FINDINGS

The concept of soul, heaven, hell, astral body; all these are there in every religious and philosophical scripture. Almost all religions have the same opinion that a physical body is not everything but some abstract existence is also there. The religions also believe that the world in which we live is very limited and there is an infinite world beyond this finite existence. Several researches, case studies and the real life experiences of the people make us believe that there is a life after death that cannot be denied and avoided. Moreover many scientists are also strong believer of life after death and the existence of the soul.

The observation of self-experiences and the experiences of other people, the opinions of the experts in metaphysical science as well as in spirituality; the experiments of medical doctors, all these evidences are sufficient to prove that there is a life after death. Even though there are different opinions and thoughts on what exactly happens with the person after death, the concept of life after death has been accepted by the people. Now the role of science starts. It is a challenge before science to prove that there is life after death. For proving this, science has to cross its limited periphery and think beyond the concrete facts.

On the basis of the above research the following factors have been found:

1. There is a continuous debate going on between physical science and metaphysical science but still science does not have concrete answers on life after death.
2. The comprehension of metaphysical phenomena such as life after death, existence of soul, is not possible through physical science, but some abstract factors need to be applied to study the supernatural things.
3. It was also found that most major religions on earth believe in life after death and they all tell the same theories

4. In metaphysics as well as in spiritualism, there are several thoughts propounded by the experts in spiritual, metaphysical, and religious studies. But the common opinion of all these people is that life exists after death.

5. There are several case studies available that can assure life after death.

6. For the deep study of such an abstract subject like death, rebirth etc., the person should not be constrained with the established religious beliefs. Self-experience and self-exploration is very important. No scientific equipment can be used for studying and proving the facts of death and life after death.

7. The experiences regarding life after death is different from person to person.

CHAPTER 11
FURTHER DISSCUSSION

Discussion

The scientific, religious, spiritual and metaphysical discussion on life after death has led to several inferences on the topic.

The first inference can be taken purely from a scientific perspective. The assumption here is that scientist says that there is no concrete evidence for the existence of the soul it may not be there. In science, there is no strong evidence for life after death. At the same time, Scientist cannot deny completely the existence of soul or life after death. In short, science has no concrete answer to this question. It is because science cannot eliminate this topic just by saying that the soul cannot be seen, touched or felt so there is no soul. Science has not yet reached this conclusion. Hence it can be said that science does not have the satisfactory answer to this mystery. Scientist has neither denied the theory of life after death, nor does they approve of it fully. Hence for unveiling the mysteries of life after death, it becomes essential to take support from spiritual science.

Though there is no proof of existence of soul and the life after death, many scientists are strong believers of religions and various religions have been practiced by them. Many great thinkers, saints and spiritual people from both east and west philosophies and religions have from time to time propounded the theory of rebirth. We cannot jump into the hasty conclusion that these thinkers, philosophers and spiritual Gurus are completely wrong in their philosophy. Almost all of them were theist and they would believe in the existence of soul and life after death. In modern time too, the scientists believe in the existence of supernatural power. Just from a pure scientific perspective it is not proved but it has been accepted by many scientists.

Even if, it is discussed from a scientific perspectives, it can be said that the human body is made up of millions of cells and the major work of these cells are to generate chemical energy and to create new cells. During death the cells start deteriorating and after the death of the person it is completely deteriorated, hence there is a probability to say that if the cells are perishable, the human existence is also perishable. But the discussion does not stop here. The question is do the cells deteriorate or they change their form. Well, according to the cycle of the nature every natural thing disposes and it can be decomposed. The cells also decompose and from the process again, the new life starts. It was the rational thoughts with the example of cell.

When we are alive, our consciousness is alive; but science cannot answer the question whether our consciousness still alive after the death as well. Scientist can just give opinions but they cannot give the concrete answers to this question. Science is no doubt the most important medium of gaining knowledge, but unfortunately, this knowledge is very limited.

Scientist are keen to accept the facts which can be proven through the method of investigation, experiments and lab testing. In research methodology, there are two types of research; one is quantitative and another is qualitative. Quantitative research is conducted through statistical and mathematical interpretation. It uses various statistical formulae to come to the final conclusion of the hypothesis. Quantitative analysis is to the point which can also be called the scientific approach. On the contrary, research can also be done on qualitative basis. It is a longer process of research as compared to the quantitative analysis. The qualitative analysis tries to analyse the data obtain from observations, and experiences. It conducts several prolonged interviews and open ended questions in which the researcher tries to gain thorough knowledge of the specific topic. Religious study is the subject where the research cannot be conducted on quantitative analysis. In research methodology, both of these researches have been regarded valid forms of research. For the study of concrete topics, the quantitative research is effective, but for abstract topics, we have to rely on the abstract information obtained during the research process.

If the research methodology has accepted the qualitative analysis method and the data obtained from personal experiences, case studies and observation is valid, the life after death theory must be accepted. It is because metaphysical science, spirituality and philosophical views generally come from the personal experiences and personal observations.

It can also be said that the supernatural phenomena do exist but scientist does not have the equipment to prove these phenomena. It does not come under the periphery of science. When scientist says that there is no evidence for life after death, the scientist at the same time cannot answer what life exactly is. Many abstract things are accepted by science then why not life after death.

It can also be said that for common man, death is a very dreadful experience because it takes away our loved ones from us forever. Death is an inevitable reality of those who have taken birth on the earth. Birth and death are the part of the cycle just like the cycles of the seasons. According to Hindu theory there are three major Gods; the trinity. Among them Lord Brahma is the God of birth, Lord Vishnu is the God of preserving the creation of Brahma and Lord Shiva is the God of destruction of whatever is created by Lord Brahma and Cherished by Lord Vishnu. Destruction should never be taken negatively; because if something is to be born, the previous creation has to be destroyed first. Hence destruction is necessary for the new life. As mentioned before there is a cycle of seasons on the earth, and after every winter, the spring is there. The same logic is applied in the life and death process of human beings and all other living things on the earth. So death has been studied and researched by several philosophers and metaphysics. This research was conducted through their own experiences and the experiences of the other people.

For the people who practice metaphysics, spirituality death is not the end of life. They believe that there is a life after death. There has constantly been a fierce debate among the scientists and the metaphysics on the existence of life after death and the existence of a psychic body within our physical body. The debate especially was fierce in 18th and 19th century, on the onset of industrialization. The scientific inventions proved some religious facts fraud and wrong. The scientists started challenging Christianity in Europe and the overall existence of God. The atheist movement called naturalism also developed which denied the existence of life after death and the existence of a soul. It became a trend to mock the existence of the soul and life after death. The fashionable people just threw away the old thoughts including the spirituality. Unfortunately they could not differentiate between rituals and philosophy and spirituality. -But in the first half of 20th century, when people came to know the futility of materialism, they started reinterpreting religion and philosophy. They came to know that science can ensure them material pleasure. Science can give them information but the real knowledge or the enlightenment of the person is only possible through spiritualism and metaphysical studies.

The metaphysics, spiritual people and the philosophers think death as a gateway to the soul from which the soul reincarnates itself for a new life. For the completeness of the life, death is inevitable. Unlike the common people, the spiritually enlightened people do not feel death as the miserable phenomenon. Various researchers look at death from different perspectives. Some researchers think that death is like a halt from which the endless journey of the soul starts. The researchers of this area have also urged people to gain thorough knowledge about this subject. Instead of being a scientific person we should try to be enlightened person.

Scientist tends to ask for concrete proof 0f the abstract phenomena such as reincarnation or the journey of soul after death. It gives importance to the concrete or physical existence of the person. The fight of scientist is basically with the restricted religious laws. Religion imposes certain rules on human beings. The person has to follow them without questioning the probabilities of those rules. But spirituality or metaphysics are different things. Metaphysics stresses on the human experience. According to the researchers of metaphysics, knowledge gaining process of abstract phenomena is subjective and each individual is given freedom to experience it.

Metaphysics is also called a science because it conducts the research and study based on observation, experiences and case studies which are the integral parts of research methodology. It gives answers to most of the questions very rationally and logically. This is what the objective of any science is there.

It is also rational to believe in life after death because the number of believers of life after death is more than the number of non-believers. If maximum number of people believe in particular thing, if some of them also have experienced something supernatural, it is not a rational idea to deny everything just for the sake of denying.

If science wants concrete evidences, the question is why does scientist says that energy exists? It should also be taken into account that scientists believe in those things which cannot be proved with the help of any apparatus or other scientific equipment. Moreover, it has been proved in physical science that there is an energy which makes things move. Otherwise each and every element of the universe would have been in a still position. The planets are moving in a disciplined manner, the animals, insects, human beings are moving from here and there. Our earth is consistently revolving around the sun. All planets have maintained a certain distant from the sun. They are neither getting diverted from each other nor are they ceasing to revolve. Behind the movements in the universe, we must admit that some power or energy is there which is controlling everything. The cycle of creation, living status and destruction is incessantly going on for millions of years in the entire universe. Hence the cycle of life and death should also be there which needs to be studied thoroughly and positively.

Though religious practitioners, philosophers, spiritual people and metaphysical scientists strongly believe in the concept of the soul, life after death and reincarnation they vary in their opinions. There are some differences about the opinions regarding what happens after death.

We have also discussed the beliefs of various religions regarding the journey of the soul and its life after death. Many experts have given a number of theories to convey the reality of these abstract phenomena's. After studying thoroughly the various opinions expressed by various religions, one of the common fact that I would like to highlight and that is the influence of Karmas on the rebirth. Karmic theory is prevalent almost in every religion and every culture and civilization. Some major religions of the world such as Hindu, Christianity, Muslims, Judaism, Buddhism, and Jainism are similar in their opinion of Karma theory. All of these religions believe in action and reaction theory. The Karma theory tells us that if the individual is involved in good activities and good thoughts, he will lead a peaceful life after death. On the contrary if the person has involved for most of his life in doing evil deeds and carrying evil thoughts in his mind will lead a very miserable life after death.

One more strong reason why we should believe in life after death or such similar supernatural phenomena, and that is the testimonials and credentials given by the great philosophers, saints, and spiritual gurus. The thinkers, philosophers like Plato, Aristotle, Socrates, the Indian philosophers like Chanakya, Varah Mihir, and many ancient Indian sages have written a lot about the existence of rebirth. Hence rebirth or life after death cannot be a myth.

REFERENCES

"BBC - GCSE Bitesize: Christian Teaching". *Bbc.co.uk*. Web. 8 May 2016.

"BBC - GCSE Bitesize: Judaism and Death". *Bbc.co.uk*. Web. 9 May 2016.

"BBC - Religions - Spiritualism: History of Modern Spiritualism". *Bbc.co.uk*. N.P., 2009. Web. 12 May 2016.

Brancaz, Steven. "Harvard Neurosurgeon Confirms The Afterlife Exists". *Spirit Science and Metaphysics*. N.P., 2014. Web. 8 May 2016.

Chopra, Deepak. Life after Death: The Book of Answers.

Dao, Ming. "The Critical Issue of Life and Death". *Buddha Net*. N.p., 1996. Web. 9 May 2016.

Donnelly, John. *Language, Metaphysics, and Death*. New York: Fordham University Press, 1978. Print.

"Egyptian Civilization - Religion - Life after Death". *Historymuseum. ca*. Web. 13 May 2016.

Fechner, Gustav Theodor. *The Little Book of Life after Death*. New York: Arno Press, 1977. Print.

Francis Crick, The Astonishing Hypothesis: The Scientific Search for the Soul (New York New York: Scribner Maxwell Macmillan International, 1994), p. 258.

"German Scientists Prove There Is Life After Death". *World News Daily Report*. N.p., 2014. Web. 9 May 2016.

Holden, Janice Miner, Bruce Greyson, and Debbie James. *The Handbook of Near-Death Experiences*. Santa Barbara, Calif.: Praeger Publishers, 2009. Print.

"Jainism Simplified Chapter 4 - Gati". *Umich.edu*. Web. 15 May 2016.

Jung, Carl. "On Life after Death". *The Nautis Project*. Web. 3 May 2016.

Katha Upanishada 1.2.5 Chapter 1, Section 2, Verse 6

Knapton, Sarah. "First Hint of 'Life after Death' In Biggest Ever Scientific Study". *The Telegraph*. N.p., 2014. Web. 8 May 2016.

Leadbeater, C. *The Life After Death and How Theosophy Unveils It*. Madras: The Theosophical Publishing House, 1952. Print.

Masters, Paul Leon. Master's Degrees Curriculum 1 vols. Burbank, CA Printing, 2012. Microsoft Word file

Shahzad, Khurram. "True Islam - Reincarnation Theory". *True Islam - Reincarnation theory*. Web. 5 May 2016.

Swami Adiswarananda,. *Hinduism: Death and Life Beyond Death. Ramakrishna.org.* Web. 8 May 2016.

Ted, Peter. *Models of Life beyond Death.* N.p. 2002. Web. 13 May 2016.

The Spiritual Bee "Life beyond Death". Web: 13 May 2016.

Weiss, Eric. The Long Trajectory: Reincarnation and Life after Death. N.P. 2009. Web: 13 May 2016.

Withnall, Adam. "Study Provides Evidence That 'Near-Death' Experiences Are Real". *The Independent.* N.p., 2014. Web. 13 May 2016.

Yogi Ramchandra, *The Life beyond Death.* YOGeBooks, 2010. Print.

ABOUT THE AUTHOR

Dr. Smith is the author of *Truth in Business and Home Lending Discrimination* and *Beyond Wisdom*. He also served as the Associate Director of Houston Allied Health Careers, a Technical healthcare institution. Dr. Smith also lectured and did consultation in business management and is the Director of New Dimension Counseling.